What Can I Do
When I Grow Up?

Published in 2019 by The School of Life
First published in the USA in 2020
70 Marchmont Street, London WC1N 1AB

Copyright © The School of Life 2019
Character illustrations © Tyla Mason
Design and illustrations by Studio Katie Kerr
Printed in Latvia by Livonia

The School of Life is a resource for helping us understand
ourselves, for improving our relationships, our careers and
our social lives – as well as for helping us find calm and get
more out of our leisure hours. We do this through creating
films, workshops, books and gifts.

www.theschooloflife.com

ISBN 978-1-912891-20-7

10 9 8 7 6 5 4 3 2

What Can I Do When I Grow Up?

A young person's guide to careers,
money — and the future

THE SCHOOL OF LIFE PRESS

Contents

What can I do when I grow up?

It's impossible to spend time with adults without one of them coming up to you and asking (as if it were the most normal thing in the world), 'What do you want to do when you grow up?' They mean for this to be a relatively simple question; the idea is that you'll quite easily be able to say something like, 'a teacher' or 'a doctor' and then they will move on and bother someone else.

What would you like to be when you grow up?

Umm.... a teacher, I think?

But the real answers to this question can be much more complicated, and if you've ever felt confused or annoyed by being asked it, you have every right. Properly knowing what you want to do with your working life is one of the biggest, strangest and hardest questions of all. It may take you decades to find a good answer to it — and it is one that most adults are still grappling with, even the ones who are already quite old and who know how to do a lot of complicated work things already (like paying taxes or managing an office). If you could magically look inside the minds of the majority of adults, you would find many of them trying to decide whether the job they are doing now is truly the one they want to keep doing, and asking themselves big questions like, 'What do I really enjoy?' and 'What's it all about?' Another somewhat strange secret is that a lot of adults do not actually feel like adults inside. They're older, of course, but in their minds, they may secretly be feeling not so different from when they were a lot younger; they might be wondering when real adult life will begin and why a lot of things don't have the neat answers they once hoped they might have. In other words, it is truly odd that this enquiry — 'What do you want to do when you grow up?' — is so often seen as a child's question when, in fact, it's a really tricky adult question that even the most serious and wise grown-ups have problems with.

In order to answer this question properly, you need to know a lot about yourself (what you enjoy, what you're good at, what excites you), you should know a lot about the world (what money is, what jobs are available, what the economy is) and then you need to somehow put the two together, fitting what you like and can do to the needs and requirements of the world. It is a very complicated puzzle, and it is true madness that adults have come to think that young people should be able to summon up a reply in a few seconds, on the basis of having been to school for a few years. We would not expect a child to know how to drive a car or build a robot without being taught how to first, so nor should we expect a young person to work out the meaning of work on their own. So this is a book that is a bit annoyed by the way that children and young people are asked about the future, and that wants you to take this question more seriously than you are normally allowed to — so that it can hopefully point you in the right direction.

A word of warning, though: we are definitely not promising you that by the time you finish this book, you'll know exactly what you want to do with the next fifty, sixty or seventy years of your working life. However, we can guarantee that you'll at least start to appreciate why the question about your future is quite subtle, quite complex and very important. The next time an adult you don't know well asks you this question, you will also have some good replies, for example, 'I don't know yet but I'm thinking about it...' And if you're feeling brave, you could add (with a smile), 'What about you, do you know what you want to do?' They might stop bothering you quite quickly after that — or it'll be the start of a fascinating conversation.

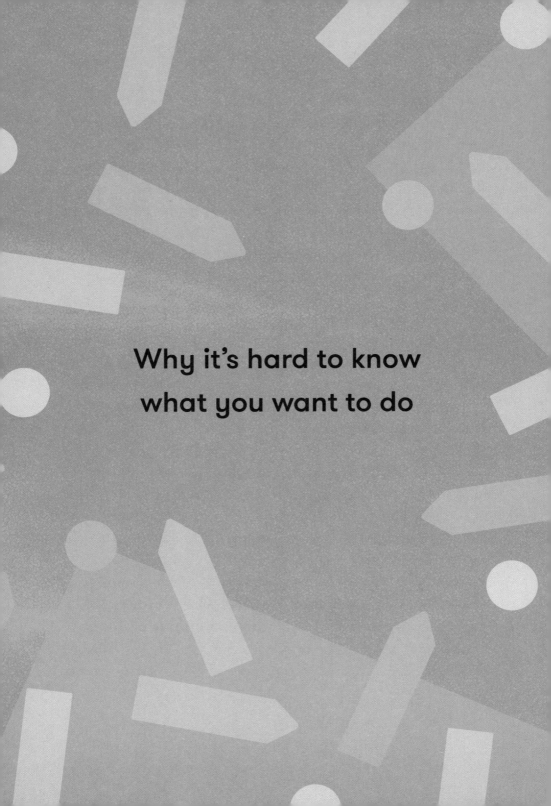

Why it's hard to know
what you want to do

There are some particular reasons why knowing what you might want to do is so difficult at this point in time. Let's look at a few of these reasons:

REASON #1

It's a new kind of question

For most of human history, people didn't go around asking, 'What should I do when I grow up?' The issue was far simpler and far more automatic: *you just did whatever your parents did.* If your parents had a sheep farm, you'd be a sheep farmer; if they were bakers, you'd be a baker; if they had a ferry across a lake, you'd have a ferry across a lake.

Even being a painter — a job that nowadays we think of as something you do because you especially love drawing — was in the past an occupation you took up primarily because your family was devoted to it. That's how it worked all over Italy at the end of the Middle Ages.

Take the Bellini family, who lived during the 15th and 16th centuries. They went into painting (doing lots of different paintings of Jesus and Mary) generation after generation, simply because that's what you did when your surname was Bellini.

Painted by Dad

Jacopo Bellini, *Madonna and Child*,
c.1465

Painted by Son #1

Giovanni Bellini, *Madonna and Child with
St. John the Baptist*, c.1490–1500

Painted by Son #2

Gentile Bellini, *Madonna and Child
Enthroned*, c.1475–85

The Bellini Family
of Painters

In other words, you never had to worry about what job you wanted to do; the issue was decided for you by the family you were born into. In some ways, that made things much simpler. There wasn't too much agonising. People did not stress that they were in the wrong job or that there might be a better job that they hadn't been clever or canny enough to think about doing. They got on with the only job that was available to them. Sometimes the fit was perfect: what their family did was exactly what they enjoyed doing. But obviously at other points, there were some unhappy matches: lawyers who dreamt of playing the trombone and trombone players who would have loved to be carpenters and carpenters who dreamt of designing ladies' handbags (we have made that one up, but you get the picture).

Incidentally, the same was true for marriage. People did not choose who they wanted to marry. They were told who to get together with by their families. Often, there was a surprise on the wedding day, because the two people getting married might have never met before then — and though there were some great matches, there would have been some grim ones, too. The key point, though, was that you knew from the start that you didn't get to choose, you accepted what was put on your plate — and you more or less got on with it.

Then, about 200 years ago (which is when historians generally think the 'modern' world began), a big new idea came into being: *that you could choose a job yourself, depending on what you liked doing and what you were good at.* Your parents might have made horseshoes, but if you preferred to write poems about daffodils blooming in springtime, then you could give that a go. Or if you wanted to be an army general, even if you came from a family that repaired lead roofs, then you'd follow your heart, join the military and learn about muskets.

Talking of hearts, the same kind of change occurred around marriages as well: suddenly, you were allowed to find your own partners on the basis of love, even if your parents thought your prospective partner was ill-suited, ugly or dangerous (or even all three). There were no more surprises on wedding days — and no more arranged marriages.

In the case of both jobs and love, there were a lot of advantages to the new system (a chance to earn money the way you truly wanted to and to spend your life with someone you actually liked) but a few disadvantages as well: what if you realised you were in the wrong job halfway through your career? What if you decided you'd picked a deeply annoying husband or wife, despite your best intentions? There would only be yourself to blame, which is always painful.

The modern world is much more comfortable in lots of ways (especially if you get toothache) but it brings with it particular kinds of pain that our ancestors never knew: first and foremost, the pain of making the wrong choice.

REASON #2
People want to be happy

Nowadays, people expect to be happy in their work — and they really didn't always. If you'd stopped a ploughman in 600 AD (about a third of the way through the Dark Ages) and asked him if he was *happy* to till the soil, he would have looked at you very strangely. Happiness did not come into it. You worked on the land because you had to, because God said so, because your dad did that and most of all, because you needed the money.

That kind of attitude tends to sound extremely depressing to modern people, who feel much more hopeful about their work. You may hear adults moaning that it's Monday or complaining that their jobs are stressful at points, but overall, in our era, people try very hard indeed to enjoy their jobs at least some of the time. No one thinks it is good enough to work just for money; that sounds really sad. Of course, money is essential to have and can make you feel proud when you earn it, but if your job is completely horrible day in, day out, then the money does not seem worth it. Modern people want to have a go at finding a job that will be fun and pay a decent wage.

That's not a silly hope to have, but we should notice that it is a very big wish and a relatively new one — which means that we're going to need a lot of help to make it come true.

REASON #3

It's hard to know what you want

A big difficulty in all this is that our brains are not very good at telling us what would make us happy. We know quickly enough when there is a problem, but that's different from knowing what we need to do to feel content.

You get a sense of this aspect of our minds when, for example, a relative asks you what you want for your birthday. You might know that there are some things you'd be happy to receive and others you'd really hate, but when you're asked just like that, straight out, your mind may go blank. It's really hard to identify a good present for yourself: you have to understand what the options are (you need to see a lot of gifts before you can know the gift that's going to be right for you), have a good sense of what you've enjoyed in the past and a realistic sum of money to play with, as well as access to the right sorts of shops. Any of those ingredients might be missing, which is why it's very rare to be given a present that actually hits the spot. And if that's the case with presents, think how hard it is with jobs, where many of the same factors apply: the same ignorance of the full range of options, the same weak hold on our sense of what satisfies us, and the same set of practical hurdles around money and access. Too often, people (by which we mean competent and serious adults) can end up thinking: *I know I want something, but I don't know exactly what I want. I know this job is wrong, but what might be a better one... ?*

At many points in the Bible and in the history of Christianity, we hear examples of God speaking to humans and sharing with them a plan for what he wants them to do with their lives. In different ways, that's what happens with Moses, John the Baptist, the Virgin Mary, St Teresa of Ávila, St Francis of Assisi and Martin Luther; one day, they all hear a voice from God instructing them that he wants them to do a specific kind of job for him on earth. It might be starting a monastery, taking the Israelites out of Egypt or helping the poor. The point is that the voice is clear, it's got a really strong view of what has to be done and it tells them that they're exactly right for the job, no ifs, ands or buts.

It's definitely an odd idea, and if you're not religious, a truly unbelievable one. However, it captures something important about the way that many of us think of the way we'll figure out what to do with our lives. At some level, we hope that we are going to wake up one day and hear a clear, authoritative voice telling us what to do next: 'You should become an accountant!' 'You need to be a dentist with a special focus on wisdom teeth and plaque,' or, 'You need to be an avocado farmer!'

Some people do seem to hear the equivalent of such a voice. The proper word for this is a 'vocation' — a 'calling' to do something with your life. From a young age, these lucky people just know what they want to get up to: they burn with a desire to play the clarinet, or they know that they want to design jet engines or start a safari company specialising in observing the kudu (an antelope with amazing curly horns that lives in Namibia).

Most of us, though, don't have vocations of this kind, and we shouldn't beat ourselves up about it. We're usually interested in quite a few things, but never with any kind of overwhelming clarity — more in a casual 'hmm, that could be fun' kind of way. A lot of things interest us, but not one area above anything else. Many adults, when they ask children what they want to do, seem to be fishing around for signs of a 'vocation', but it's a strange thing to look out for, given how rare it is (probably one in 1,000 of us has one). Almost no one, of any age or any size, has any kind of overwhelming vocation and that's more than fine. It's no sign that you're going to have a dull or uninspiring life, just that you're going to need to work at finding out what you might do — which is completely normal, and very doable.

REASON #4

The work question isn't given enough attention

Deciding what to do for work is one of life's big tasks. You'd therefore expect that a lot of time and money would be devoted

Safari Guide

A specialist profession for those who love animals and being outdoors. Requires a sense of adventure and an appreciation for wearing binoculars.

to helping people figure out what jobs they might do. Perhaps there would be colleges where you can do a course on 'How to Find a Great Job that's Just Right for You'. Maybe there is a university somewhere out there called the 'What to Do with Your Life University', where there are specialist professors with whom you can study for a few years and come out with all the right answers about your future.

But the truth is that mostly our society just doesn't admit how tricky it is to decide what jobs we might do, and therefore does not make any of the large-scale arrangements that would be necessary to help us. We're mainly left alone — and that's why a lot of unnecessary mistakes happen. There is a strange contrast between the huge amount of attention people give to training you how to do a specific job, and the tiny amount of attention they give to helping you to figure out what job, out of all the thousands of options, you might want to do in the first place. All the training is in jobs, not in the *choice* of jobs.

Suppose you decided you wanted to be a pilot. No one would expect you to become one quickly, or just work it all out for yourself. There are lots of great courses and schools and plenty of instructors to take you on training flights, and only after many years would you eventually be ready to be in charge of flying a passenger plane to Berlin or Canberra. But there's none of this kind of in-depth help and instruction around the actual decision of whether to become a pilot (or, perhaps instead, an insurance salesperson or a legal secretary). You don't have years and years of classes on 'how to decide what to do' and careful practice courses where you can try out different scenarios and get a sense of what it's actually like doing different sorts of jobs. You're expected to step into the cockpit of life and know how to fly. That's a real pity — and that's why we've written this book.

REASON #5

You don't see how adults got jobs

Some of the reason why, as a young person, the world of work can be a bit confusing is that by the time you've arrived on the scene, the adults closest to you have probably worked out what they're doing job-wise — at least in some ways. So it can seem as if something that's very unclear to you is just naturally clear to the people you love most; they just happen to be in 'travel' or in 'sales' or 'working in the council office'. But how did they get there? How did they know this is what they wanted to do? A lot of that got worked out before you were born, or when you were very tiny and now, without meaning to deceive you, the adults just don't manage to explain the path they took to be the sort of people they are today.

But if you start to study any adult's path, what's striking is how haphazard and meandering it often is — in a way that should give you hope, because it means that you too will be able to wander around and get a bit lost for a long time and yet things will come right nevertheless. You do not have to work it out the minute you finish school or university. You can end up in a satisfying destination that you did not for a long time even suspect existed.

Imagine someone aged 45 with a rather interesting job in a supermarket chain. Probably when they were eight, they had no idea what they wanted to do; and when they were 16 they craved to do all kinds of things that were very unconnected with their later occupation: maybe they wanted to be an environmental scientist, a guitarist, or to work in television.

But when they were 20, they realised that it would not be easy to do any of those things. At 21, they worked for a year in a sportswear shop. Then they went travelling for a year (to Mexico and France). Then they worked with some friends in a small business selling books about dogs. That business did not go very well. To make the books they had to get a photographer to take photos and the photographer happened to have a brother-in-law who worked in a supermarket.

As the dog-book business was failing, this person then applied for a training course, and after that, they were placed in charge of people stacking the shelves in a supermarket. They had to make sure that the shelves were always full, even though people were constantly picking stock off in irregular patterns. They did that for a year, then they were offered a position at the head

Supermarket Logistics Manager

Do you like neatness and order? Are you interested in finding patterns in people's behaviour? If so, managing the logistics for a supermarket might be an interesting career for you.

office near Swindon, where they managed 20 supermarkets. Then 30. Then last year, they moved into their present job looking after the supply of all of the soft fruit throughout the business (soft fruits are things like strawberries, raspberries and blueberries — but not apples or pears).

If you met this person, they would look rather confident and able to speak with great authority about what they do. But they weren't born this way — they didn't hear a voice from God telling them to handle the flow of blueberries from southern Spain into the UK; they just meandered around, and that is eventually where life took them.

That's very often the way it is. Very few of us have a plan, but almost all of us — in the end — find a destination that fits, more or less.

REASON #6

Most books are about something else

There are few books out there helping you to know what you might do when you grow up (we checked). There are more books about dragons than there are about finding the right job — and even more on dinosaurs. That's understandable, but it's a good idea to start turning over this question in your mind every now and then, in a casual way, so that you'll never be unpleasantly surprised. Not least, you will have something a bit unexpected to say the next time an annoying adult comes up to you and asks, as though it were the simplest thing in the world, what you might like to be one day when you're older.

For this first activity, write down what kind of job or jobs you think you'd like to do on this piece of paper (you can leave it blank if you're not sure yet!). Try not to think about it too much — just write down the first thing that comes into your mind.

Once you've finished the book, come back to this page and see if you have changed your mind. Or if you left it blank you'll hopefully have some ideas for what you might want to do in the future.

What I might like to be when I grow up:

_____

_____

_____

_____

_____

_____

_____

_____

_____

_____

_____

_____

_____

_____

_____

_____

_____

_____

_____

_____

_____

_____

_____

What is a job?

This could sound like an obvious question, but what exactly is a job? What do all the varied things that people do 'for work', from writing contracts for a shipping firm to taking out small children's tonsils, have in common? The simple answer is: *a job is something you get paid for doing.*

That may sound pretty obvious, but it actually leads straight to a very big and tricky question: *Why do people get paid to do things?*

You may think people get paid for doing certain things because they take a lot of effort. But that's not quite right: there are lots of things people do that are pretty hard but that they do not get paid for. For example, you have to go to school and do a lot of work, but (sadly) you don't get paid for doing that. You might try very hard to get good at football, but you don't get paid for your efforts; if you climbed up a mountain, it would take a lot of sweat and tears, but you wouldn't receive a salary. So it can't really be that people get paid because they have to make an effort.

The real reason you can get money for working is this: *People pay money because they have a problem that they cannot solve on their own.* They need someone else to help them — someone they generally do not know and who can't just do it as a 'favour' — and they have to hand over some cash in exchange for their assistance. The more urgently and desperately they need the problem solved, the more they may be willing to pay (especially if there are few others on hand to help). It's a big idea: *work is about solving other people's problems in return for money.* Jobs involve helping people out, not out of love or friendship, but in order to be repaid in money. Or as it's sometimes said (to draw attention to the way that every kind of work is helping to straighten something out for someone), we're all doing each other's laundry. To get the hang of this idea, let's look at a few jobs and see what problems they are solving for other people. It's not always obvious.

Dry Cleaners

Let's go back to laundry (it's a surprisingly interesting topic). Some clothes are quite hard to clean, especially something like a smart woollen suit or a silk dress; you can't just put them in the washing machine, because they'd shrink and discolour. You have to use special equipment that people do not have at home and chemicals like tetrachloroethylene (which gives dry cleaning shops their funny smell). An entire industry has grown around the fact that people will occasionally spill wine down their front or get a pomegranate stain on their trousers. Millions of people around the world make their living removing little bits of goop from cotton and woollen fibres.

One of the largest dry-cleaning machine companies is called Renzacci, who are based in the middle of Italy, in a place called Città di Castello. One of their best machines is called the Planet 150 Industria, which costs more than the average car and will sort out almost any kind of stain in the world.

It's almost beautiful what the problem of stains has given rise to, when you think about it.

Pizza Delivery

It's not really all that hard to make a pizza, but it can be very inconvenient to have to make one yourself when you have to do homework as well — you might be hungry *and* busy. The problem that needs to be solved is: *how do you get something nice to eat without having to stop what you are doing?* A lot of jobs in the modern world are not solving complicated problems. They're helping us with pretty basic inconveniences that delay and frustrate us — and they involve finding faster and better solutions than those that were around before.

All those motorbikes and mopeds zooming around the world's cities late at night in the rain, carrying pizzas in a box in the back, are all in the business of solving the problem of how to keep doing something urgent while quietening the rumbles of hunger in your stomach.

Psychotherapists

Many jobs need complicated equipment in order to do them: drills, computers, lenses... It can sometimes seem as if what defines a job is the command of some kind of technology. But that isn't true either. Take the job of being a psychotherapist — someone who listens very carefully to someone else's problems and gives them wise advice and helpful encouragement. You don't need any fancy equipment to do that — just two chairs in a comfortable room — and yet still, people will hand over money to psychotherapists for the basic and simple reason we have already identified: because they are being helped in ways that they couldn't help themselves. You give money in exchange for sentences like, 'Maybe you should take the time to explain to your partner how you really feel when they tell you they're unhappy.' (Perhaps your parents might have been to a psychotherapist, it's a very interesting and worthwhile thing to do.)

Some people might say that psychotherapy doesn't sound like a 'real' job, but we are learning that a real job is simply one where money is exchanged in return for help, in whatever form that help is needed.

Professional Football Players

Why are a few lucky people paid to play football, when almost everyone else who plays isn't? Why is football sometimes a job and sometimes just a hobby? This gets to the heart of what work really is. Football is a hobby when it is fun for you. But football becomes a job when the way that you play starts to matter a lot to other people; so much so that they'd be willing to pay you in order to watch you handle the ball in certain ways. The highest-paid footballers are ultimately those who are best at solving the problems of the greatest number of onlookers:

Psychotherapist

A trained professional that serves their clients in profound ways.
If you're a good listener and curious about human behaviour,
you could help people overcome all sorts of problems.

the problem of these onlookers being that they really want their team or their country to win and would be deeply sad and hurt if they didn't.

We should say a word here about what a 'problem' is in this context. Most jobs are solving an easily identifiable problem. A baker is solving the 'I'm-hungry-at-tea-time' problem. The dentist is solving the 'my-back-tooth-hurts' problem. And the footballer is also solving a problem, but it's perhaps one that is less easy to see or define. We might put it like this: the top footballer is solving the 'I'm-desperate-for-my-chosen-team-to-win-this-Saturday' problem. It may not feel like an urgent or overly serious problem, but it really is for some people, and that is why football clubs will give talented players a lot of money in exchange for help with it — which is in turn what transforms a hobby into (for a tiny minority) a highly lucrative profession.

Songwriters

At first it also feels difficult to say what problem a songwriter is solving. But think about a song you really like. It is giving you feelings that are important to you: it can make you feel happy, excited or maybe sad in a really interesting way. The song helps you to feel better at moments when you'd otherwise feel bored, confused or without enthusiasm. So, just as with a baker or a dentist, a songwriter is solving a problem for you — and you would be willing to give them hard-earned money in order to help you in ways you wouldn't be able to help yourself.

Songwriter

Do you love to make music? A songwriter creates songs for themselves or for others to perform. There's no guarantee that it will pay well, but it could feel both meaningful and pleasurable.

There are so many ways that people need different kinds of help; from everyday problems (like getting stains out of your clothes) to trickier ones (like being able to open up about your inner worries and fears). If you think about it, almost all jobs have an element of helping others or solving problems.

Think about the kinds of jobs your parents, aunts and uncles, older siblings or even your neighbours do for a living. Imagine them at their job and do a drawing of them working. Can you guess what kind of problems they are solving with their jobs?

This is:

_____

when they are at work.
The problem they are
solving is:

_____

_____

_____

This is:

_____

when they are at work.
The problem they are
solving is:

_____

_____

_____

This is:

_____

when they are at work.
The problem they are
solving is:

_____

_____

_____

Why are there so many different jobs?

One of the most striking things about the modern world — and a big reason why identifying the right job for yourself is so difficult — is that there are simply so many different types of job that you could potentially do. In Europe in the year 1500, it's estimated that there were only 400 different jobs to choose from; now there are over a million.

Back then, the main job was farming. More than half of the working population was in some way employed in agriculture. Other jobs included being a sailor, a weaver, a stonemason, a carpenter or a shoemaker. These jobs were fairly easy to understand and directly related to something you could see, touch, wear or eat. If you lived in a village or a town, you'd spot the blacksmith working in a shed (which would probably be on the main road); you would see the farmers ploughing the fields and stonemasons building walls and houses. If someone mentioned a job, you'd almost certainly know immediately what was involved.

But in our times, there is an apparently infinite variety of jobs and many of them are very hard to make sense of. For example:

Cloud Chief Architect

This is someone who designs the way in which a company might store its important information on computers that are not actually in the company's buildings, but connected to them by high-speed cables.

Investment Analyst

A person who provides research about the financial status of companies, sectors and nations for people looking to make money by lending it to others.

Immunologist

Someone who investigates disorders of the human immune system, and works to reduce rejection by the body of newly transplanted organs.

Logistics Coordinator

This is someone who organises the transport of goods, with a particular focus on their price and speed.

Quantity Surveyor

A person who tries to work out how much concrete or bricks or glass are going to be needed in a new building, and how much these will cost.

Procurement Clerk

The person in a large company in charge of ordering the raw materials used in the production of goods.

Cloud Chief Architect

This might sound like a dreamy and fantastical job title but it is actually one that requires a lot of technical knowledge and a methodical mind.

Actuary

Someone who works out the risk of all kinds of catastrophes unfolding, for companies and individuals.

Epidemiologist

A specialist who investigates diseases not in individuals but in large groups: an expert in the spread of viruses and bacteria through air and water.

The biggest reason why there are so many jobs is something called *specialisation*; modern workers are, above anything else, *specialists*. That is, they know a lot about doing one fairly small thing, they are highly trained in it (perhaps they spent years at university learning all about it) and they are very efficient at their tasks.

In a specialised world, you will find one person in a factory who only thinks about the best way to add a layer of foam to a mattress, or one person in an office who will spend all of their day worrying about what to do when customers call up and complain that their packages are late, or one person whose entire job is to check the tyres of cars that have been rented out to holidaymakers (someone else checks the bodywork, etc.)

Epidemiologist

An epidemiologist studies the patterns, causes and effects of diseases. If you're interested in the health of people, this might be an option for you. Requires an analytical and curious mind.

This wasn't always the way it was. For most of history, people were *generalists* — that is, they might grow a bit of food in the morning, then work at making a chair at lunchtime, then do the accounts at teatime, then sew some clothes in the early evening and finally make some candles just before bedtime. There was definitely a lot of variety and it must have been fun to have a go at so much. But it was also, interestingly, desperately inefficient, because someone who does many things quite well is unlikely to be very brilliant at doing any single one of them (as the expression goes: *jack of all trades, master of none*).

Imagine if you had to do a bit of brain surgery, but also bake bread and fly a plane and write songs: all these activities are fascinating, but you see why someone who does brain surgery every day is going to end up much better at it than someone who also has to make loaves of sourdough and land an Airbus every now and then.

In the 18th century, a great Scottish economist called Adam Smith first thought about just how difficult, slow and wasteful it can be when you try to do everything, and he recommended that, in order for a country to grow really rich, people should stop trying to do a bit of this and a bit of that and instead focus on one task only, done all day, month in and month out. What gave Smith this idea was a visit he made to a superb new and efficient pin factory near his home in Edinburgh. Smith was amazed by how specialised all the jobs in it were, and as a result, how much work got done. He wrote about it in his book.

One man draws out the wire, another straightens it, a third cuts it, a fourth points it, a fifth grinds it at the top for receiving the head.

To make the head requires two or three distinct operations; to put it on is a particular business, to whiten the pins is another; it is even a trade by itself to put them into some paper.

The important business of making a pin is, in this manner, divided into about eighteen distinct operations, all performed by distinct hands.

I have seen a factory where they could make upwards of forty-eight thousand pins in a single day. But if they had all worked separately and independently, and without any of them having been educated to this peculiar business, they could have made perhaps not one pin in a day.

— Adam Smith

From Chapter 1 'Of the Division of Labour', Book 1 'Of the Causes of Improvement in the Productive Powers of Labor', *An Inquiry into the Nature and Causes of the Wealth of Nations* (1776)

Not one pin a day! Adam Smith was very clever. He correctly spotted that doing one job, preferably for most of your life, makes you very good at it. And so factories and offices become super efficient when they are filled with people whose whole job it is to do things that might, earlier on in history, have been mere moments in an average day.

Specialisation is why nowadays, in rich countries, we have all ended up studying hard in pretty narrow fields of work and then taken on weird-sounding and very specific job titles like Senior Packaging and Branding Designer, Intake and Triage Clinician, Research Centre Manager and Transport Policy Consultant. We have become tiny cogs in giant efficient machines.

Ideas and thoughts

In many types of work there's the option to be a specialist or a generalist within that area depending on what you are most interested in.

For example, say you would like to be doctor. What kind of patients would you like to work with? A doctor that helps children is called a *paediatrician*, while a doctor that helps older people is called a *geriatrician*. Or maybe you don't care about how old your patients are and you're only interested in a specific part of the body like the brain (a *neurologist*) or the heart (a *cardiologist*). The doctor that you've probably had the most experience with is known as a GP in the UK. GP stands for *General Practitioner*. Because they are 'General' Practitioners they know lots of different things about people of all ages and different parts of the body, so they can help with coughs and back ache or that weird rash on your finger — but if something is really tricky, they will have to refer you to a specialist who can look into the problem more closely.

Think of a field of work that you might be interested in. Try to note down all the different smaller, more specialist jobs that might be involved in that area of work.

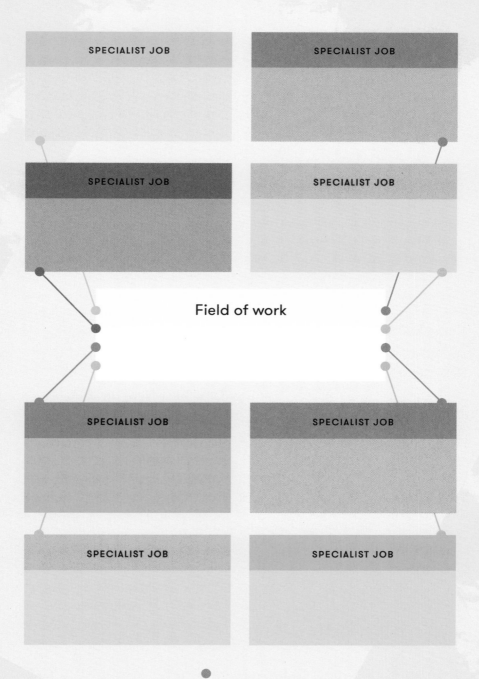

SPECIALIST JOB

SPECIALIST JOB

SPECIALIST JOB

SPECIALIST JOB

Field of work

SPECIALIST JOB

SPECIALIST JOB

SPECIALIST JOB

SPECIALIST JOB

Why some jobs can
be a bit boring

Doing one narrow job all your life is definitely the best way to get as good as possible at it — and therefore to make the most money from it. But that still leaves one important question: what is more interesting, to be a specialist or to be a generalist? And here the answer is more complicated. The truth is, it is probably more fun to be a generalist — and the way you can tell is by looking at the way that most children will naturally spend their days playing.

Very few children ever decide to devote all their time to only one kind of game. Variety is a good deal more interesting. So in a single Saturday morning, as children, we might put on an extra jumper and imagine being an Arctic explorer, then have brief stints as an architect making a Lego house, a rockstar making an anthem about cornflakes and an inventor working out how to speed up colouring in by gluing four felt-tip pens together. Afterwards, we might put in a few minutes as a member of an emergency rescue team, then try out being a pilot brilliantly landing a cargo plane on the rug in the corridor. Then we'll perform a life-saving operation on a knitted rabbit and finally we'll find employment as a sous-chef helping to make a ham and cheese sandwich for lunch. Each one of these 'games' may be the beginning of a career — but it is a whole lot more fun doing them for ten minutes at a time rather than solidly for fifty years. Less efficient, but more fun.

Compared to the way children play, most adults have no option but to lead pretty restricted lives. A doctor may dream of writing poetry but she probably won't have time to do so, because she'll have many patients to see and articles about new medicines to read. A pilot might long to bake cakes but his main job will be flying to another continent, which gets in the way of producing tarte tatin (a caramelised apple tart from France). It does make us all richer and more efficient to be specialists, but it can also be a lot more boring.

One of Adam Smith's most intelligent but critical readers was the German economist Karl Marx, a man who was — among many other things — the inventor of an economic system called communism. Marx agreed entirely with Smith's analysis of efficiency; specialisation had indeed transformed the world and possessed a revolutionary power to make individuals and nations richer. But where he differed from Smith was in his view of whether or not this was a good idea. We would certainly make ourselves wealthier by specialising, but Marx passionately pointed out that we'd also make our lives really boring. And he firmly believed that it was better to have an interesting life than a very wealthy one.

In Karl Marx's ideal society, he proposed that everyone would have lots of different jobs — even if it meant people being a bit less efficient and therefore less rich. There were to be no specialists here. In a pointed dig at Smith, Marx wrote in his book *The German Ideology* how it is nice to do lots of different things without needing to specialise.

In communist society... nobody has one exclusive sphere of activity but each can become accomplished in any branch he wishes... thus it is possible for me to do one thing today and another tomorrow, to hunt in the morning, to fish in the afternoon, rear cattle in the evening, criticise after dinner... without ever becoming a hunter, fisherman, shepherd or critic.

— Karl Marx

From *The German Ideology*, 1846

There's no right or wrong way here, but the choice (Adam Smith for the specialist team, Karl Marx for the generalist team) is one worth thinking about when we plan our lives.

The truth is that you can still — even nowadays — have the working life of a generalist. If you fancy it, you could, in a single day, work on making a chair, bake three cakes, write poetry and grow some plants. You could even do ten different jobs over a lifetime, but you might get paid less and be less good at doing each one of them than someone who focused early on on a single career. But that might be a price you'll think is worth paying for the sake of having something else that's very important in any life: fun.

What we are learning is that earning money is not the only thing we want from work. We also want work to be interesting. Sometimes adults use the word 'meaningful' to describe the best kind of work, and what they mean by this is work that helps other people in some way, either by reducing their suffering or increasing their pleasure.

Interestingly, the vast majority of businesses do help people in some way — otherwise they'd go bankrupt. However, crucially, a great many jobs are in the odd situation of *being* meaningful while not in any way *feeling* meaningful. They're worthwhile but they don't feel worthwhile. Frankly, they're a bit boring and the reason comes back to our friend *specialisation*, along with another problem, *scale*.

Cake Baker

A cake baker specialises in creating sugary delights. Make no mistake though, being a baker is tough — you need a head for numbers as well as making things look and taste delicious.

Most modern businesses are on a very big scale. In medieval England, the average business employed four people. Today, most people in England work in companies of over fifty people. A sizeable chunk are in companies of over 1,000 people.

Furthermore, these big companies move slowly. They do not decide on a product on Monday morning and have it ready by Tuesday afternoon. They might do some careful research for eight months, then spend two years making prototypes, then one year building a plant, then a further six months advertising and marketing the product. That's an awfully long time to stay interested in anything, even the most gripping activity. It can be hard to stay motivated and curious when you're one person in a team of over 20,000 employees working on four continents pushing forward a project that might be ready in five years' time at the earliest.

Some of the reason why it's fun to watch a game of football is that the whole thing happens quite quickly. In ninety minutes, twenty-two players can take us on a really exciting adventure on a single pitch with a single ball and two goals.

If football were like modern work in terms of scale and pace, a game would unfold on eighteen pitches with about twenty balls and hundreds of players kicking around for thousands of days without any real feeling of progress or results and with few opportunities to even touch the ball. No wonder adults sometimes get bored — and enjoy sport on the weekend.

It isn't that their work is meaningless, it's just that everything is happening pretty slowly and the ball isn't being passed to them very often.

How do jobs get invented?

G iven how many jobs there already are, it might seem as if those that currently exist probably won't be added to very much in the future. But a striking thing about the world of work is that new kinds of jobs are being invented all the time — and are going to keep being invented far into the future. That's because a job simply involves (as we've seen) one person helping to fix a problem for another — and the good news (for those who care about being employed) is that people have a lot of problems, large and small, which ingenious people are always going to find new and better ways of fixing. We'll only stop inventing jobs when we have solved all our problems... which is not going to happen any time soon.

Let's look at examples of new jobs that have recently come into being because humans have identified new sorts of problems and new ways of fixing them. For a long time, dog owners didn't worry too much about the state of their pets' paws. If these dogs had slightly broken or unsightly nails, no one really minded. But then certain people started to point out that bad nails really were a problem for dogs, and that the problem could be fixed by taking a dog to a special salon, where the nails could be filed down and treated with ointments. So now, in cities all over the world, you'll find dog pedicurists who will offer to beautify your pooch's paws.

Or perhaps take the issue of not having anything tasty to eat. You might have thought that this issue had been solved, but not quite. Some people get bored with the fruits that are presently available in supermarkets, and are hungry to try out something more interesting. Happily for them, there are people in Peru who have focused on harvesting fruit called the lucuma, which looks a bit like a mango but has a custardy taste rather like maple syrup. All over Peru, the lucuma is used in desserts, and produces very delicious ice cream and cakes — and now the taste for lucuma is going global. In just a few years, the lucuma business has exploded. Planes flying from Peru bring the fruit by the crate-load to sell at fancy delicatessens in Sydney, New York and London, and chefs have been able to create fabulous lucuma sorbets, cakes and milkshakes.

The name we give to someone who invents new jobs is:

An Entrepreneur

An entrepreneur is someone who spots a problem, develops an idea for how to solve it and then makes sure everyone knows about it. Perhaps one day you'll become an entrepreneur. If so, what you will need above all is a really good insight into other people's problems. Of course, you'll also need to know about money and working hard — but really, what you need to be above all is a problem-spotting expert. Whenever you spot a problem that's not being solved — in your own life or the lives of others — you are also spotting a new business waiting to be developed.

Dog Pedicurist

Pampering pooches' paws might not seem that meaningful,
yet it involves helping others while also making things beautiful.
Identifying a problem can be the start of a booming business.

One way to think about what businesses the world still needs is to run through an average day and ask yourself whether you can identify, in any area, problems that aren't currently being addressed. There are a few fields where business is already so well developed, there really seem to be no problems at all left to solve. But in many other areas, untreated problems — large and small — exist in every direction. We face lots of situations where we'd ideally like a solution and none seem to exist, at least not in a form or at a price that suits us: maybe we've had a furious argument with our friend and there's no one to help, or there aren't any Chinese restaurants nearby that are vegetarian, or we really need a machine that can automatically write a thank you letter to our relatives and there isn't one yet.

The biggest source of insight into the sort of problems that a good business can be built around is usually simply… you. It is from close observation of the problems you have personally encountered that a robust business has a chance to emerge. The best way to understand the needs of millions of potential customers is to understand your own needs first and foremost. The smartest form of 'market research' is looking inside you.

A big reason why certain businesses go bankrupt is that they have failed to properly identify real problems that real people have, at least on a scale necessary to support a business. You must have seen clothing shops or restaurants go bankrupt, and the reason is usually that they haven't worked out quite what their customers actually deeply want. They have made a guess, but it wasn't quite good enough (maybe customers are wanting lighter, cheaper meals and a restaurant is serving unhealthy, expensive food; or people want clothes to relax in and a shop wants to sell them fashionable but very uncomfortable items). The consequences of not guessing right can be brutal.

Governments often want to encourage their people to become entrepreneurs, as that helps the whole country to get richer, and in order to do so, they send them on courses to learn how to handle money and do accounts. That can be helpful, but the really important thing you need to know how to do as an entrepreneur is to answer three questions:

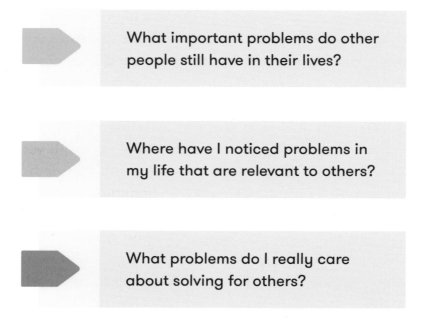

What important problems do other people still have in their lives?

Where have I noticed problems in my life that are relevant to others?

What problems do I really care about solving for others?

Airlines compete to
offer cheaper routes
to more places
all over the world

Help people understand
why they want to travel
and where it is most
helpful for them to go

Restaurants go to a lot
of trouble to offer you
interesting things to eat

Help with having a
good conversation
over dinner

Wedding planners
help people with cake,
flowers and a seating
plan for their wedding

Help people work out
who they should get
married to (quite a few
people make mistakes)

There are millions of
things to watch online

Help with spending
your time wisely

One of the interesting things about the invention of jobs is that if you look across history, you can see that the sorts of problems that jobs have solved over the centuries have changed.

Early in history, most jobs were solving 'body' problems; that is, problems connected with having a body: how to keep warm, how to stay dry, how to have enough to eat, how to feel cosy in a bed. But more recently, more and more jobs have started solving 'mind' problems, like how to be entertained, how to be calm, how to have interesting ideas to think about. Having a calm mind is not less important than having a sandwich, but it's just that entrepreneurs have not yet focused as much on issues of the mind, although they surely will in the future. One big idea about the future is that more and more jobs will be to do with helping us have happier minds.

We have learnt that a great source of ideas about new businesses lies in what you find is a problem in your life.

Take a few moments to consider the gaps you know about and then think what new businesses might be able to plug them. Use your imagination; the answers should ideally sound quite surprising!

What's missing in your life:

What kind of business could solve it:

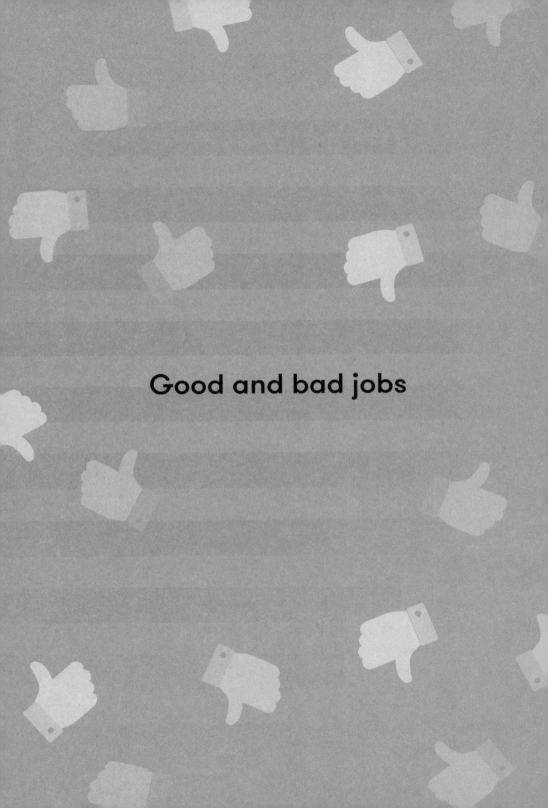

Good and bad jobs

Normally, when people speak about a 'good' or a 'bad' job, they're referring to how much it pays. So a job in a bank is often thought of as 'good' because it pays a lot while a job in a factory is considered 'bad' because it doesn't. But there is another, more fundamental and perhaps more interesting, way to distinguish between good and bad jobs. In this view, what makes it good or bad is the seriousness and importance of the problem that the job is trying to solve. A job becomes *good* the more it solves a problem that really matters, and it becomes *bad* the more the underlying problem it addresses is trivial or indeed positively harmful.

So a job encouraging people to smoke cigarettes that cause all sorts of illnesses is, in this sense, not really good compared to a job like being a fitness trainer who helps people get active and agile — even if both jobs pay the same amount. Or a job making television game shows where people are forced to be quite mean to each other isn't as good as one that opens their eyes to how fascinating ancient history can be — whatever the respective salaries on offer happen to be.

Most business people think that this kind of distinction is not important: all that matters for them is whether money is being made, not how it is being made. But it is really important to look at the 'how', because a good country is one in which the maximum number of people are solving important rather than slightly silly problems (not just one that is rich).

The fact that you can make money in unhelpful or nasty ways comes down to a strange fact about human beings: we don't generally have a solid grasp on what our important problems really are. We are convinced that a lot of things are important that in fact are not — and we can forget what our important problems are when people around us keep talking about the trivial ones. So someone with a bit of skill could convince us that it is really important to buy a sports car with leather seats and a turbo engine when in fact, a simpler car with a basic engine is probably just as good and we could use the leftover money to try to learn a foreign language or help a friend with their education. Or we could be talked into going to a really expensive theme park to bond with our siblings when in fact, our real problem as a family is that we don't talk to each other enough, so we might be better off taking a walk in the woods, which costs nothing.

Governments are always worrying about how many people are unemployed in a country. Being 'out of work' is a serious thing, but it's also important to think about whether people who do have jobs are well or badly employed. For example, an adult who tries to get children addicted to sweets is employed, but they are not making any real contribution to human happiness. A person who asks the government to reduce the tax on sugar might have a high-paying job, but it's not a 'good' job.

Probably most of us, when we do start to work, are going to want to do a job that will help people with genuine problems. Though money may be nice, just as important is the wish to

Fitness Trainer

Are you a good teacher? A trainer isn't just extremely fit, they also need to motivate and encourage people when they would probably rather be watching TV or eating pizza.

contribute to people's happiness. It would be pretty depressing going to work every day in a job that you know is negatively impacting people's lives. Adults will sometimes speak of their wish to 'make a difference'; that is, to come home after a day of work feeling that they have helped other human beings to be that bit less unhappy in some significant area: that seems incredibly important.

Economists and governments tend to think a lot about how to reduce what they call 'the rate of unemployment'; that is, the number of people who don't have a job. And in order to do this, they often encourage shoppers to go out and spend more money, so that businesses will get more cash. Though this can work, the method fails to draw any distinction between good and bad reasons to spend money and therefore between good and bad jobs.

Fortunately, there are real solutions to bringing down the rate of bad jobs. The trick isn't just to get people to spend money; the trick is to excite people into buying things that really matter and give these shoppers a genuine chance of happiness — for example, encouraging them to buy psychotherapy rather than guns or dancing lessons rather than cigarettes.

And for this to happen, people need to think really hard about what stands a chance of making them happy — and also, to pay a bit more attention to one thing in particular: *adverts*.

Ancient History Documentarian

Mad on mummies? Potty about pyramids? Or is there another historical period that you love? Either way, you will need an inquisitive nature and ability to weave a compelling story.

Take a look at these five different jobs. How do you think these jobs might impact the lives of others (either directly or indirectly)? Do they help people in meaningful ways?

How does a mechanic impact the lives of others?

_____

_____

_____

_____

_____

How does a barrister impact the lives of others?

_____

_____

_____

_____

_____

How does a gym trainer
impact the lives of others?

_____
_____
_____
_____

How does a pro surfer
impact the lives of others?

_____
_____
_____
_____

How does an ornithologist
impact the lives of others?

_____
_____
_____
_____
_____

Why adverts matter

This is a book about what you might do when you're older, but we're going to take a little detour to look at a question that is secretly rather relevant to all of this — the business of advertising.

Probably from when you were very little, you've noticed adverts all around you. They're on the back of buses, on television, on displays by the side of the road, and even all over the Internet. Advertising is the thing that businesses use to try to persuade customers to buy their products; they tell the world about what they have to offer. Some adverts are extremely simple. They just say: 'here's some bread and it costs this much' or 'come and buy a pair of scissors at our shop, we close at 6pm'.

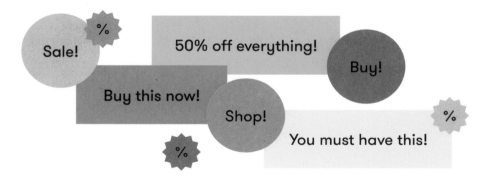

But most adverts are a lot fancier and rather cleverer than that. When you watch television, often you can't immediately tell what an advert is for. It's lovely to watch but you don't know what you're being told to buy. In one advert, maybe a family is walking on the beach, the kids are having fun and the parents are holding hands; it is a happy scene and there's lovely music and the scenery is stunning and it's pretty exciting to watch. You know it's an advert — you don't know what it's for but it must be for something delightful. Yet at the very end, you're suddenly told that it is an ad for an expensive bottle of perfume from France called 'Sea Air'. Hmm!

Adverts can cost companies a lot, and the reason why people pay to get them made and displayed is because, mostly, they actually work. Customers change what they think they want according to what adverts they have seen. You might have no idea that you ever needed a certain kind of toy or car or piece of clothing or perfume, but then you see one in an advert and you start to want it very badly.

But how do adverts persuade you to want things so urgently? In order to convince you, adverts will do something extremely clever that you should look out for in the future: they focus on something we all really, really want — something very basic and essential that you can't actually buy, like a happy family, or a feeling of calm, or a sense that someone loves you — and they show it to you in a really beautiful way so that you start to ache for it and then, at the end, just when you're really on their side, they tell you about their products, which might be pretty boring or useless things, like a credit card, a fancy watch or a handbag. The idea is that you get profoundly excited for something you really want (like a feeling that someone cares for you) and you become almost hypnotised, and then next thing you know you

Advertising Creative

Do you like working out what makes people tick? Are you persuasive with creative flair? Working in advertising can be a lucrative career.

are trotting off obediently to a shop or bank, to get that credit card or buy that gold watch. But, of course, it's not going to give you that happy feeling you are after because credit cards and golden watches are quite boring. In other words, adverts often sell us things we don't really need by waving in front of our eyes things we do really ache for.

Now you know this, in order to make sure you don't fill your life with stuff you don't really need, a big question you should ask yourself before shopping is:

> Do I actually *need* this
> or do I simply *want* it?

There can be a big difference between *wanting* something and *needing* it. We can be deliberately confused by clever adverts.

If you want to get a sense of the awesome power of advertising, just go around your house looking for things that no one cares about any more: kitchen gadgets that haven't been used in ages, games that no one looks at, abandoned clothes and perfume bottles. It is no coincidence that these are in your house: many of them were bought because an advert made people feel they were a very good idea.

What's all this got to do with jobs? Well, in a perfect world, adverts wouldn't be so sneaky. We'd be making and selling each other things that we do really need — and adverts would be telling us about them honestly rather than exciting us about stuff that's not important. Many businesses already do this: they do a great job of selling us important products that make a genuine difference — but some businesses do not. In your future, you might want to think about trying to find a business to work for that makes stuff people do in fact deeply need.

And, in the meantime, you might want to keep a careful eye out for adverts that promise you something amazing but then sell you something that ends up being a bit unloved in the back of a cupboard.

In the last chapter, we have learnt about the distinction between things we *want* and things we *need*.

Think about how that might apply in your own life. We've made a few suggestions to get you going.

THINGS I MIGHT WANT

A greasy cheeseburger
from a local fast-food
restaurant chain

The latest smartphone
with inbuilt cameras
and facial recognition

Some recently released
special-edition trainers
that cost a small fortune

THINGS I ACTUALLY NEED

A healthy meal you've
learnt how to cook that
will make you feel good

Your first film camera
to start a hobby for
amateur photography

Some comfortable and
affordable trainers for
playing football well

Visible and invisible jobs

One reason why it is hard to know about all the jobs that exist is that many of them are slightly hidden from view, which can be a pity as some of these hidden jobs might be ones you would like to do.

We can distinguish between 'visible' and 'invisible' jobs. The visible jobs are related to stuff that you can buy: jobs that go towards making things like newspapers, food, houses, cars, clothes or computers. Because everyone can see, touch and feel these products, many people will think of getting jobs making them, which means there can be a lot of competition for these positions. A slightly frightening number of people want to be architects or chefs or journalists or fashion designers, more than there's actually room for in the world.

But actually there are lots of other jobs that not many people think about because they're one step removed from the end product. These are the jobs involved in making stuff that no ordinary person goes into a shop to buy: like a wind turbine or a submarine. Think of a phone. Everyone knows the big brand names that make new phones; every year, millions of young people try to work for the companies that produce them.

However, there are lots of much more invisible jobs that are involved in building bits that go inside the phone that very few people think about — things like the memory chip, the antenna, the microphone, the circuit board and the battery.

You can have a very interesting life working in the invisible jobs that are behind the scenes and one step removed from what's in the shops: you could, for example, work for a battery company or an antenna company or a circuit board manufacturer that most people will not have heard of but that are fascinating, friendly and growing fast.

The way that we refer to the difference between invisible and visible jobs is with slightly strange acronyms: B2C and B2B.

B2C	B2B
means 'Business to Consumer'	means 'Business to Business'
is related to stuff the public buys	is related to stuff businesses buy
are jobs that are 'visible'	are jobs that are 'invisible'

Wind Turbine Engineer

An 'invisible' job designing and maintaining very visible devices that convert the wind's power into electricity. Could be a career for those interested in renewable energy and technology.

B2C stands for 'business-to-consumer' — in other words, a business that will deal directly with shoppers and ordinary members of the public (people that get called 'consumers'). Whereas B2B stands for 'business-to-business', and refers to jobs where you're making something that you're only selling to another business (and that you'll never see in a shop, like a wind turbine). So making antennae for mobile phones is a B2B activity, whereas selling the finished phones themselves is a B2C business. Or making a newspaper is a B2C business, but making gigantic vats of wood pulp is a B2B business. Or making car batteries is a B2B business but selling electric cars is a B2C business (because an ordinary person can't buy a car battery, only big businesses will).

The reason why it is important to understand this distinction is because B2C jobs can get a bit too much attention. People don't often use their imagination when wondering who to work for: they like reading magazines, so they imagine they want to work for a magazine. They like eating in restaurants, so they decide they want to open a restaurant. But by keeping in mind that there are lots of very nice 'invisible' jobs, one step removed from the everyday shopper, you'll be increasing your chances of finding something that may be worthwhile, comfortably paid and pretty interesting as well.

Electric Car Salesman

A 'visible' job selling energy efficient vehicles to customers.
You'll need to have good technical knowledge about cars,
as well as being a confident and persuasive speaker.

As we've learnt, B2C stands for 'business-to-consumer', a job that deals directly with members of the public, whereas B2B stands for 'business-to-business', and this term refers to jobs that deal with other businesses.

To help you get the hang of this distinction, take a look at these lanyards and decide which people have jobs that are B2B and which are B2C. Circle the answer.

NAME
Sandy Digger

JOB
Iron Ore Miner

B2B   OR   B2C

NAME
Pāni Strokes

JOB
Swim Teacher

B2B   OR   B2C

NAME
Clementine Ng

JOB
Pastry Chef

B2B OR B2C

NAME
Manuel Ventura

JOB
Office Manager

B2B OR B2C

NAME
Ryan Spelt

JOB
Wheat Farmer

B2B OR B2C

NAME
Melody Piper

JOB
Singer

B2B OR B2C

Why do some people get paid more than others?

One of the things that we quickly realise about the world of work is that not everyone gets paid the same amount. Two people can work for roughly the same number of hours, both can be clever, diligent, well dressed and hard-working — and one will make about 300 times as much as the other. That seems very confusing and perhaps rather unfair too. How is this possible?

Sometimes, in the modern world, we're encouraged to think that people who earn a lot of money are very good people and those who earn very little are pretty bad. Money can seem like an indicator of whether you're a decent person or not, which is why many people who don't earn very much get quite sad and have trouble respecting themselves, which is heartbreaking. Not only do they have a modest salary, they also have the feeling that they aren't very important or good because of it. At the same time, you sometimes hear the very opposite being said: that people who earn a lot are plainly bad people who are greedy and nasty and selfish, whereas poor people are the good ones — and that can be pretty harsh as well.

Is any of this correct? Are the rich 'bad' and the poor 'good'? Or vice versa? Which one is it?

The truth is actually a lot simpler — and in order to understand it, we have to go back and think about what a job is (which we were discussing earlier on). Let's remember: a job is something you do to fix a problem for someone, and money is what you get in return for fixing it. Now, the reason why people get paid different amounts of money is rather simple: it is because not everyone is as good at fixing problems as everyone else. Some problems are so tricky, they can only be fixed by certain people who have a rather rare talent or skill, whereas other problems are much more straightforward and can therefore be fixed by lots of people. This has an effect on salary: the more people can fix a problem, the less each of them will be able to ask for in order to fix it; and the fewer people that can fix a problem, the more those who are able to fix it will be able to extract. That's why a singer who produces unusually catchy tunes and hits all the right notes will be paid lots of money whereas someone who makes very tasty and wholesome sandwiches won't (because lots of people can do that); or a brain surgeon will have a high salary and a skilful and careful bricklayer won't.

Before we go any further, we should quickly notice something crucial: differences in salary will say nothing necessarily about whether a job is 'important' or not; it simply says something about how badly customers want a problem fixed and how rare the skills to fix it are. Let's compare two people: *someone who can kick a ball 60 metres into a goal* and *someone who can look after a patient in a hospital who is suffering from cancer.*

The footballer might be paid a fortune, and the nurse hardly anything. Yet this has nothing to do with whether or not the footballer is fixing a really important problem; it is just that enough people want the goal-scoring problem fixed in relation

Professional Footballer

Can you curve a ball into the back of the net to score a winning goal in the 90th minute? Not many can, which is why playing professional football is only an option for a talented few.

to the number of people who can fix it and so the salary goes up and up (sometimes to millions a week). Similarly, helping someone with cancer in a hospital is obviously a worthwhile thing to do, but it's just that this is a problem that a lot of people can actually fix — and therefore, hospitals can get away with paying nurses very little.

We often behave as though money tells us if we are good or not; another way to say this is that we interpret salary 'moralistically' (we say that there is a 'moral' to the story of the high or the low earner; we are on the lookout for baddies and goodies). But that's not right. That is not how money works, as we have learnt. Salaries are not decided by whether someone is doing something 'important' or not; salaries are simply the result of the intensity with which certain people want a job done, relative to the number of people who happen to be able to do it. If many people can do a task, however important it might be (holding a hand on a cancer ward), little money will be offered for it. But if there are very few people who can do it, however trivial it might be (playing football very well), if there's a sufficiently intense demand, salaries are going be high (and the footballer can buy an expensive Italian sports car).

Money is not really an accurate measure of how good or bad someone is. It just reflects the strength of demand for a job in relation to the supply of workers who can do it. Or to put it simply, how much people want something that not very many people can do.

Nurse

Being a nurse isn't always well paid but it gives you a chance to help people in a number of meaningful ways. It requires empathy, resilience and the ability to work as part of a team.

You'll hear a lot of people arguing that the world should be 'fairer'. By this they often mean that everyone should be paid roughly the same. Whatever you think of this idea (Karl Marx, who we mentioned earlier, was very keen on it), it isn't going to happen any time soon. The present system is too deeply fixed; it would be like trying to change the weather.

However, if you are upset about the differences there are in salaries today, you can make a change easily — and do it right away. You can change what you think money *means.* You can move from thinking that money tells you whether someone is good or bad to thinking that it's something far less important. You can understand that it reflects *the strength of demand for a job in relation to the supply of workers who can do it.* You don't have to think that people who are nurses in hospitals aren't important or that footballers are amazing. Or vice versa. You can make your own mind up without thinking about money all the time.

This can be very useful, because one day, you might have to make a choice between a job that pays a lot and a job that pays not so much. You might think the job that doesn't pay as much is pretty interesting and would be fun — but you might get sad when you learn that it doesn't pay very much, and you might feel like you don't want to do that job because your friends won't respect you if you do not earn more. But this chapter should have allowed you to look at the choice a bit differently. No job is bad simply because it doesn't pay much or good because it pays a lot — or the other way round. Money isn't given out that way. Realising this means you'll have more options to play with when it comes to choosing a job. And in the meantime, you'll be able to think a bit differently about nurses and football players.

Take a good look at all these different kinds of jobs. Without thinking about how much they will be paid, circle which jobs you would most like to do.

When you are done, think about what you chose and why you chose it. Are you surprised?

STORE MANAGER

MECHANIC

ARCHITECT

BARRISTER

ART HISTORIAN

COUNSELLOR

WRITER

TECH ENGINEER

SCIENTIST

MUSICIAN

VET NURSE

ECONOMIST

CAFE OWNER

PARAMEDIC

SPORT COACH

CONSERVATIONIST

SURF INSTRUCTOR

PRO ATHLETE

How important is money?

It can seem as if, when you are an adult, you should always try to make as much money as possible. But as we're coming to see, it might be that sometimes you will decide willingly, with your eyes fully open, to earn less money in exchange for something else, like for example:

More fun

More time with your family

More of a sense that you're doing something 'meaningful'

Money may be very, very important (because of course we need money to pay for important things), and at the same time, not the most important thing in the world.

You can get a sense of this by doing a little thought experiment. Imagine if someone offered to pay you millions every year, but you had to sit alone in a room doing Latin verbs day in, day out. Or, imagine if you were paid a very low salary (but enough to buy food and somewhere simple to live) and yet you could have fun all day. Which would you choose? The answer seems obvious. What all this means is: you can't really say that making a lot of money is the same as having a 'good job'. There are some quite bad jobs that might make you unhappy that will pay very well, and there are some good jobs where you are doing something very nice for other people and having fun yourself, but that do not pay much at all.

Suppose, for example, you got a job as a lawyer. You'd have to spend your days in meetings with people trying to understand very complicated problems of law. You'd have to sit at a desk most of the time, reading a lot of documents very carefully, and putting aside your own ideas about what's right or wrong or good or bad in order to win your case. You would need to follow exactly what the law says, even if you don't think it is a very good law. You might find that fascinating — or you might find it boring and frustrating. If you don't like it — if it doesn't suit you — you'll be spending hours and hours every day for many years doing things you can't stand. You'll probably make quite a good amount of money but you will likely end up feeling very unhappy and wondering how many more years there are until you can retire.

When you think about a job that pays well you may be thinking mainly about all the nice things you could buy with the cash. But it's easy to forget that you would actually be spending most of your time doing things that you don't enjoy at all. At which point you might need to question what the point of the money really is. It's not that making money is bad, it's just not the most important part of a job. What you should try to look for is the kind of job where you could be doing something that makes you *enough* money, but that also provides you with something you enjoy doing.

Lawyer

Are you persuasive and persistent, with good people skills? Lawyers also need to be able to understand complicated documents with technical legal jargon.

How much money is 'enough', then? It's normally assumed that it's always better — if possible — to have more money. That sounds obvious. But maybe it is not. Let's ask a really strange-sounding but serious question: *why is it nice to have more money?* The main idea is that you can have a nicer time if you have more money. But — very surprisingly — that's not totally true. How much you enjoy your life isn't really all that closely linked to how much money you spend. The connection between fun and money is quite wobbly.

Take an example that might not feel terribly important to you at the moment but often matters a lot to adults: going out for dinner. You could go and eat at a very cheap restaurant — they won't be serving interesting food and the dining room might not be particularly nice. Or you could pay much more and go somewhere elegant and eat very elaborate dishes. Which is the better experience?

A lot of people think it is obvious. Of course it is better to go to the expensive restaurant; that is why it is good to have more money. But actually the answer isn't obvious at all. Suppose you went to the cheap restaurant with two or three really lovely friends and you had a very interesting conversation, everyone laughed a lot and you had a feeling that you were loved and appreciated; you'd have a wonderful evening. But if you went to the expensive restaurant with someone you didn't like and couldn't think of anything interesting to say to, you'd have a miserable evening (even though the food might be delicious).

What this means is that having a good time depends on other things — not just on how much money you spend. You could have a great time in the expensive restaurant as well, but only if you had the right friends and the right conversation — and that's telling us something very important: it's the friends and the conversation that are making the difference, not the food!

Or what about going on holiday? Imagine that you are offered a choice between staying in a luxury hotel where you can go jet-skiing and scuba diving and there's a go-karting track in the grounds. It's going to cost a lot of money. Or, you could go camping, where there won't be any amazing activities, but it won't cost very much money. Which one is the better holiday? A lot of people would immediately think the expensive holiday would be better. But actually it's not so obvious.

What we often find is that what makes the difference between an OK holiday and a really good holiday isn't how much it costs, but what else happens: do you make a friend? Are your parents getting on? Do you do fun things in the evening? All of these things aren't really dependent on money.

What is true for holidays or dining out is true for life more generally. A good way of thinking about money is to see it like an ingredient in a meal: it's an important ingredient, but you can't make anything good with it just on its own. Just as you need olive oil to make lots of nice dishes, but if you only had olive oil to eat, you'd feel miserable and sick.

Does money help you have a better holiday?

DISAPPOINTING HOLIDAY IN AN EXPENSIVE HOTEL

You feel lonely and your parents aren't getting on. Jet-skiing is fun for a bit but you would rather be doing it with a friend.

GREAT HOLIDAY IN AN EXPENSIVE HOTEL

You all get on. You go on some exciting day trips and play fun games in the evening. There is a nice family staying nearby and you make a friend.

DISAPPOINTING HOLIDAY IN AN INEXPENSIVE CAMPSITE

You feel lonely and your parents aren't getting on. Exploring the beach is interesting for a while but you would rather be doing it with a friend.

GREAT HOLIDAY IN AN INEXPENSIVE CAMPSITE

You all get on. You go on some exciting adventures and play fun games in the evening. There's a nice family at the campsite and you make a friend.

Around money, the other key ingredients you need to be happy could include:

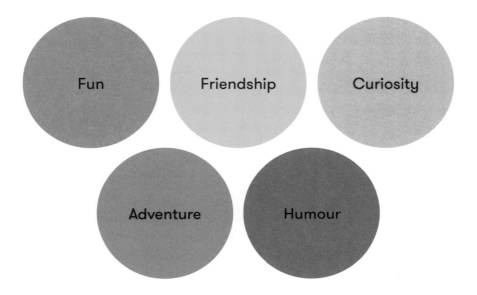

If you've got these things, you will probably have a good time even if you haven't got very much money. And if you haven't got these other ingredients, it doesn't matter how much money you have, you still won't have a very enjoyable life. Once again, this is something to consider when picking a job. There is no point earning a lot of money if you're going to be miserable in a hundred other ways. And similarly, if you're going to be having fun in a job, you really won't mind so much if you have to go and spend your holidays in a tent.

Let's have another look at the key ingredients you might need to be happy in your career. Which of these things do you think would make you happiest? You could try ranking these in order from 1 to 6.

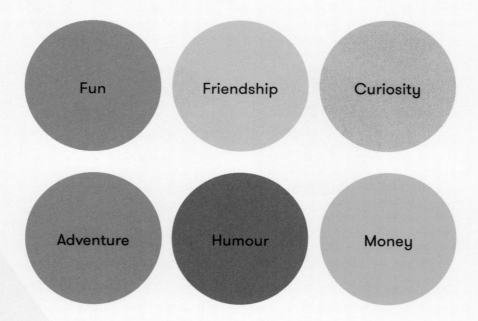

Fun

Friendship

Curiosity

Adventure

Humour

Money

Once you have thought about what would make you the happiest, you can now think about what jobs might have those key ingredients. For example, if you ranked Adventure and Curiosity as the most important, you could write down jobs like an archaeologist, a travel guide or a captain of a container ship.

The key ingredient/s that are important to me are:

1 _____   4 _____

2 _____   5 _____

3 _____   6 _____

Some jobs that might have these ingredients are:

_____

_____

_____

_____

_____

_____

_____

_____

_____

_____

_____

_____

_____

_____

_____

_____

_____

_____

What makes a job enjoyable?

We have learnt that making money is an important part of having a job, but that getting paid isn't the same as actually enjoying what we do at work. So what are the other things that can make jobs interesting and satisfying? What is 'fun' and 'meaningful' at work?

Helping people

As we have already seen, one of the basic reasons why people enjoy their work is that they like helping other people. This sounds a bit strange because we're used to thinking that we like getting things out of others. But it truly is often far lovelier to feel you've helped someone than to have received something from them.

Maybe a friend was a bit worried and you said something that cheered them up, and you felt a special glow at having been able to change the way they felt. Or maybe one day you made breakfast for your mum and she was extremely pleased with the way you laid out the dishes and brought up the tray, and that was an amazing feeling for you, even if it was quite a bit of work. Strangely, it can simply be a lot more fun giving someone a present than receiving it.

Some jobs don't really help people at all. Suppose you worked in gambling. People who gamble on football matches or horse races almost always get it wrong and end up losing money, and then deeply regret having wasted their money. If you worked in gambling, every day you'd know that there were lots of people getting more and more unhappy around you. It could slowly drive you mad.

Therefore, one of the first things to ask of any job is not 'How much does it pay?' but 'How does it help others?' In asking this, you're not being a saint. You're focusing on yourself in the best way — because as properly wise people know, pleasing others really is a joy.

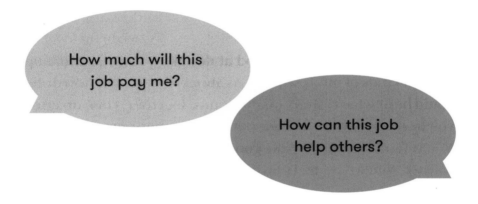

How much will this job pay me?

How can this job help others?

Using your skills and abilities

Imagine you are getting dressed — but you are only allowed to use one hand. It's an intriguing challenge at first and it is possible. But after a while it's frustrating. It seems so silly not to use your other hand. This little thought experiment is telling us something important. We get frustrated when we can't make use of our abilities.

This can happen at work. Suppose you're really good at arguing —you like working out why something is right, and you are good at finding reasons and explanations. Not all that many people are good at this. But imagine you had a job where you weren't allowed to argue — you just had to agree with people (if you were running a hotel, for instance, it wouldn't be a good idea to argue with the people staying there). It would be like having to do everything with one hand behind your back. And imagine, by comparison, the joy of taking a job in politics, where arguing is what you would try to do every day. At last, you'd feel you were free to be yourself.

Or suppose you are really good at design — you can come up with all kinds of interesting ideas about what shape something could be or what colours might be nice together. Then imagine you have a job where no-one cares about these sorts of things. You would feel that a really good part of you wasn't needed or wanted. You would feel crushed and overlooked. Whatever the money was like, you'd be dying inside.

The things we are good at aren't accidents. They are connected to the unique ways our brains works; they make every one of us different and special. The trick to finding a good job is therefore to know more about our sources of pleasure and talent.

It's impossible to say what a good job might be for everyone in the world. It all depends on the intricate fit between your skills and the needs of the world. And so the challenge is to stop

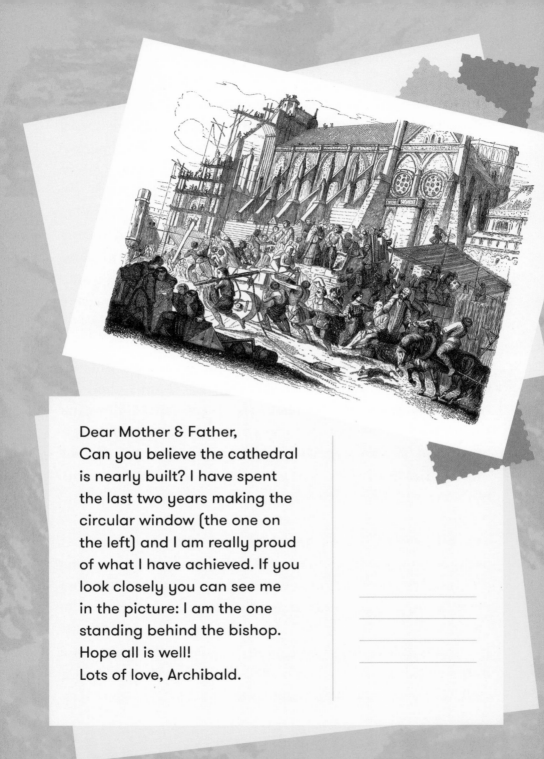

Dear Mother & Father,
Can you believe the cathedral is nearly built? I have spent the last two years making the circular window (the one on the left) and I am really proud of what I have achieved. If you look closely you can see me in the picture: I am the one standing behind the bishop. Hope all is well!
Lots of love, Archibald.

thinking about what a good job is in general, and to start to think about what a good job is 'for you' — in other words, what your particular tastes, talents and interests are.

Seeing the result of your work

Imagine you lived a long time ago and worked on the building of a cathedral. It would have taken a very long time to build and hundreds of people would have been employed to make it. Maybe you spent years helping to build the roof or you designed and made just one of the windows. You'd only be making a very small part of the building, but you could see how what you were doing was important. All the effort you were making (going to work when it was cold, getting tired, getting dust all over your face...) would result in something you could see and that other people could admire. You'd feel proud of what you had done (even though you'd only done a small part). You'd feel a sense of *accomplishment*.

That feeling tends to be very important at work. It can happen in lots of different ways. Perhaps a teacher might feel a sense of accomplishment when a pupil reads a book on their own for the first time. Or someone who has started a business shaping surfboards feels a sense of accomplishment when a champion surfer chooses their equipment. Or an inventor of electronic gadgets might feel a sense of accomplishment when they see a group of kids playing with one of them in the park.

A big requirement of work is a feeling that it's all adding up to something that you can step back and be proud of: that you've had an impact, however small, on the world; that you're leaving things better than when you started.

From this, we can put together a very broad idea of how work in general is enjoyable, even if we can't say exactly what the perfect job is for you...

WHAT IS A GOOD JOB?

A good job is one in which you will be using a range of skills and abilities that are important and particular to you, in order to help people to be slightly less unhappy or slightly more thrilled and excited. In a good job, you'll be able to step back when you retire and see that your efforts really have made some kind of difference, even if it's a small one, in the lives of others.

Surfboard Shaper

Do you love to catch a wave and are you good with your hands?
This specialist profession combines a love of the outdoors,
the pleasure of beauty and technical skill.

What do you really enjoy?

One of the more dangerous ideas that people have about work is that it should, if it is done right, be really rather unenjoyable. Work should be about suffering. That sounds very serious — but it's also profoundly wrong.

The people who are really good at their jobs, who do well at them and who help others as part of their jobs, actually enjoy them quite a lot. Indeed, you can't do a job well unless you're having fun, because only when you enjoy it do you bring all your energy to bear on it and give it everything you've got.

Jobs done out of duty, in order to please someone else (like your parents or your bosses), are never going to be as productive and accomplished as those done out of love. Your occupation as an adult might not feel amazing every single day but it should generally — if things are going OK — be pretty nice. Misery is not what adult work should be about.

This means that you need to take both your pleasure and your happiness very seriously. Thinking about pleasure is central to achieving a good working life. This idea sounds odd only because schools almost never think about fun. Fun does not come into it around school work: you're meant to suffer — or so it can seem on a bad day. However, your ability to do your job properly as an adult is going to depend on you getting a good sense of what actually brings you joy, and then finding a job that matches.

However, this swiftly brings us to a problem that we've been circling already in many sections of this book: that it isn't easy to know what we actually enjoy. It should be, but it really isn't. We all find it very hard to give a detailed account of what's truly fun and interesting for us. You get a sense of this issue if you've ever been asked why you enjoyed a funny film. You know the film was hilarious, but it can be really difficult to explain why you laughed as hard as you did. We're much better at feeling pleasure than at understanding the reasons for it. Our minds aren't good at knowing the origins of their joyful feelings. We know fun when it happens, but we can't easily step back and get a solid sense of why it occurred.

Still, we can make progress, so long as we understand that it's going to be a bit of a challenge. We have no option but to try to get to grips with what we enjoy; we're going to need to get serious about fun.

Rail Logistics Engineer

If you like order, technology and being on time then you might be on the right track for a career in rail logistics.

The best place to start is to take a deep breath and make a list of all the things that feel like fun. It could be anything: going snorkelling, running, playing card games, listening to music, watching the sunlight on the window blind, drawing an imaginary world, dressing up like a pirate, stacking plates, playing with your brother, cooking lasagne, talking quietly to your grandmother... Don't worry if it sounds weird or unimportant or if it only seems to appeal to you: for example, setting the table nicely, cleaning a cupboard, imagining living somewhere else, making soup, or drawing pictures of animals. If it's a pleasure you feel, write it down.

Next, let's ask an unusual but very important question: *what is it you like about what you like?* In other words, try to dig deeper into your pleasure. Don't just say that you like something, but try to find a reason *why* you like it. We've got you started with some examples.

Once the exercise is done, the column to focus on is the one on the right, because that is the one that contains the pure essence of what's fun for you. What is written on the left is where you happen to find pleasure, but what is written on the right is what the pleasure actually is — and that is a far more useful kind of knowledge.

WHAT I LIKE DOING:

Building cities out
of Lego blocks

Drawing pictures
of leaves that have
fallen off trees

Chatting with my
little brother

WHY I MIGHT LIKE DOING IT:

Imagining better ways
for people to live together

Finding something beautiful
and then holding on to it by
studying it closely

Teaching someone younger
than me interesting things

The great discovery to make is that your pleasures exist in more places than where you may have found them to date — and they exist both in childhood games and adult jobs. It isn't that adult jobs are exactly like games, but rather that the pleasures can be — beneath the surface — remarkably similar. For example, the pleasure of imagining a better way for people to live can exist both in an adult job like politics and a childhood game like Lego. Because you found the pleasure in Lego first does not mean that is where it has to remain or what it has to be limited to. Adults are sometimes a bit too literal in this area — they don't always get the different meanings that pleasures can have. They might see a child enjoying playing with Lego and immediately think that this means the child should become an architect, because that seems as if it would be the adult version of Lego. But if you look at it more deeply in terms of the pleasure involved, you'd find that a child who enjoys Lego could have a great time doing any number of jobs that involve planning a future for people: it might mean working in the government, or arranging what equipment an army will need, perhaps being in an engineering firm, or calculating how many trains are going to be required in a decade's time on the coastal branch.

What we're discovering is that the pleasures you enjoy when you're younger are very likely to be the same sort of pleasures that you're going to enjoy in your work as an adult. However much knowledge you're going to acquire in the years ahead, and however different you may seem to be (taller, with more wrinkles, and much more serious-looking), in important ways, you'll be the same 'you' as you are now, and your pleasures are going to be remarkably similar, too. Hints of what you should do in later life are therefore definitely present already in the things you like doing right now, it is just that you shouldn't be too direct and literal in building a bridge between today and the future: do not think that you are going to want to do the exact same grown-up version of the thing you do now. That is, a love of baking biscuits doesn't have to mean you'll want to run a biscuit factory or a love of playing football doesn't mean you will want to be a footballer. It's more that the underlying pleasures you're engaging with now should ideally be the ones that you look for in an adult job. All this explains why, if an adult is feeling bored in their work and can't think of what to do that would be more fun, one of the best questions you can ask them is: 'What did you enjoy doing as a child?' The answer is going to be full of clues as to what they might do next.

There are thousands and thousands of possible jobs out there for people to do, but once you start to whittle this vast pool of jobs down and look for the pleasures that underpin them, there are far fewer of them that will be the right fit for you. We think there might be twelve really big pleasures in life — and all of these are already present in lots of the things that young people naturally love to do.

Take a look at the pleasures listed on the next few pages and see if any of these ring a bell. If they do, it might begin to answer the question of what you might like to do as an adult.

The Pleasure of Making Money

You loved the time when you made biscuits to sell at a stall; it wasn't the money, it was the excitement of seeing that people really liked what you'd done and were happy to prove it to you by giving up something valuable. The next time you added different coloured icing, and it was fascinating to see which colours people went for and which didn't go down so well.

For you, money is appealing not in and of itself. It's interesting because it's a reward for understanding something about other people.

You really love making things attractive and tidy around the house.

You have a watch that you like because the strap had an interesting pattern: green with red squares in a line down the middle.

You enjoy wrapping birthday presents for your parents very carefully and get bothered when you can't fold the ends neatly.

You envy a friend's bike because the wheels are an unusual size and this suits their personality.

At school you take care when underlining the title of an essay; one year you experimented with wavy lines, at another point you used a ruler and obsessed about the thickness of the line; sometimes you spend so long getting the title right you don't have much time left for actually doing the writing.

You notice when two buildings are misaligned, it spoils the street and you wish someone had taken more care and noticed how jarring the junction is; you wish you could go back in time and put it right.

The Pleasure of Creativity

You like opening Lego and scattering bricks all over the floor; you love all the possibilities of the lovely things you might make from the rubble.

You love cutting up cardboard boxes. There was a memorable time a washing machine arrived in one so big you wanted to live in it; you made a window flap and stocked it with blankets, pillows and a bar of chocolate.

You sometimes wish your favourite songs were a little bit different — maybe they should repeat a particularly nice bit, or make their voices go down instead of up at the end; you would like to fiddle with it (even though it is lovely already).

Before you go to sleep you imagine other things happening to your favourite characters in a story; how would it have been if they hadn't missed the train, and had maybe a whole set of other, possibly even more interesting adventures?

You bother your parents with questions: why are birds called 'birds' and not something completely different? What would chimpanzees look like if they were shaved? Do they have time on other planets? You want there to be good reasons for things.

You were shocked when you realised your father could not really explain why plugging in the hair dryer made it work — how could something coming out of the wall force the little fan to turn around?

A friend once said she was jealous of her sister and that's why she was nasty to her and you were entranced by the way that this could make sense of why someone could get mad with someone else.

At school you hate it when the maths teacher says she can't tell you at the moment why this way of tackling a problem actually works and that all you need to know is that it does; you feel cheated.

You often feel people don't explain properly or they don't seem curious about the multiple possible explanations about why people act as they do. You want to know a lot more than you're told.

The Pleasure of Self-expression

You like it when adults ask your opinion (though sometimes you get frustrated because you don't know what your opinion is, but you really would like to have one).

You want to make sure you are noticed, perhaps more noticed than your little sister.

You get frustrated when people don't listen — you want to make them pay attention.

When you do something, especially when it is really good, you want it to be obvious to others that you have done it.

When you were in a play at school you loved the way you could expand on a bit of yourself by playing a character.

10

The Pleasure of Technology

Your aunt gave you a set of screwdrivers arranged according to size from micro to jumbo; you hardly ever use them but you love the sense that each one is designed to tackle a slightly different problem, which sadly rarely comes your way — though there was one lovely moment when there was a problem with a hinge on a kitchen cabinet door and your mum said, 'Where's that little set of screwdrivers of yours?' and you found one that fitted exactly (it was a 3 mm Phillips head).

You've started taking a interest in cars. When you were younger you took them for granted — but now you think of them as machines. It is amazing that these metal boxes are decked out with special dials and little screens and windows that — unlike at home — will open at the touch of a button. You are intrigued by exhaust pipes and radiator grills, which hint at the strange needs of the machine.

You hate it when people associate the future with jetpacks. It'll be far more interesting than that.

The Pleasure of Helping Others

In make-believe games, you really like rescue scenarios; like if someone is going to be eaten by piranhas and you pull them back onto the raft (which is actually a sofa) just in time.

You enjoy it when friends tell you what is bothering them. Quite often you don't know what you can do, but you really like trying to say comforting things to make them feel better.

Your father sometimes gets frantic when he thinks he has lost the car keys; you like being the one who can calm him down and say 'think, what did you do when you came home yesterday evening?' Once he found them in the bathroom.

10

The Pleasure of Leading

You don't just want to be in charge, you actually *like* being in charge (it is a difference that struck you early in life).

Lots of people at school want to be picked as the team captain but they do not really like the responsibility, they just want the status.

What you want is the job, the role, the chance to put your ideas into practice.

You enjoy it when others turn to you for advice. You don't just say whatever comes into your head, you want to solve their problems. You want them to be able to trust your judgement.

You read a story about a general in the army who surrendered to save the lives of his troops — they didn't win the battle, but he was a real leader.

When other people get in a panic you find yourself getting more focused; you like that about yourself.

10

The Pleasure of Teaching

If someone makes a mistake you really want to help put them right straight away.

You have a lovely teacher; she knows how carefully you listen and how hard you try (even if you sometimes get things wrong).

You love the feeling of equipping somebody else with your knowledge, and how you can turn their panic and frustration into mastery and confidence.

You know you have to be careful when you deliver your 'lessons'; people do not like to feel insulted, but you like nothing more than filling in the gaps in the knowledge of others.

When you're doing homework you like making your writing clear; if you have to rub out a mistake you are careful that the rubbing out is not visible. You hate making mistakes in ink and experimented once with pasting an extra bit of paper on top of a mistake to preserve the overall look of neatness.

You're fascinated by the cutlery drawer; you love the fact that everything has a special place. It bothers you that your sister does not care and sometimes drops a spoon into the fork section.

Even if you aren't much good at science you find the periodic table strangely alluring; you enjoy the idea of everything being sorted into neatly arranged elements.

You like arranging sets of pencils according to the colour spectrum... though there always seem to be some problems; does yellow shade into white or into light green (via greenish yellow?).

You get annoyed when people jump around telling a story: *'Oh I forgot to mention...'*

You can't bear how so many windows do not open.

It is lovely to get down on your hands and knees and look closely at a hedgehog or a snail. You like imagining its life, which seems as interesting as any human's.

You love camping, especially if the weather isn't perfect. It's an interesting challenge to put up a tent in a storm.

You were on a long walk in the country and it started to rain. Everyone complained, but you didn't care; you drew up the hood of your jacket, and liked the feel of raindrops on your nose.

You have mixed feelings about watching David Attenborough documentaries: you find them interesting but you don't just want to watch them sitting on the sofa with a plate of fish fingers on your lap. You want to be there in the swamps of the Serengeti plains during the wet season or clambering over the rocks of the Galápagos Islands; you would not care if you got mud up to your knees or scratched your fingers quite badly.

The Pleasure of Independence

You like getting up very early before anyone else is around so you can follow your own projects in peace and quiet.

For you, growing up has been all about getting away from people who can control you.

You like being alone; boredom rarely troubles you.

You've been accused at times of not being a team player and — to be honest — there is a degree of truth in the criticism.

You were extremely excited when you read a story about a guy who had quit his work in a bank and started a company that imports carpets from West Africa.

/10

Did any of these spark a feeling of 'That's me!' or 'I know that feeling!'? It's important to remember that these pleasures exist in childhood and in adulthood. What you find fun now can be part of your working life even as a grown-up:

If you enjoy *The Pleasure of Order,* you might enjoy being an accountant or a warehouse manager.

If you enjoy *The Pleasure of Helping Others,* you might run a care home for the elderly or train as a psychotherapist.

If you enjoy *The Pleasure of Self-expression,* you'll find it in jobs like being a company manager or advising a client in advertising.

Go back through each pleasure and give it a mark out of ten according to how much you like it and how strongly it rings a bell and then, if ever you're feeling lost about your job as an adult, come back to this book and see what you wrote. It might be a map to what to do next.

Too often, because young people don't get told enough about the world of adult work, they end up thinking they're going to have to be either an astronaut, a footballer or a popstar — which is exciting and depressing, because we know deep down that almost no one ends up doing these jobs.

Almost certainly, you won't be any of those things, but that's not to say you won't be having a great deal of fun: working life is going to be a lot more interesting and a lot more doable than you might ever have suspected, so long as you make sure to take your childhood pleasures with you.

How is work like school?

W hen you go to school, one of the big ideas that teachers will always suggest to their students (either indirectly or sometimes quite forcefully) is this: *people who work hard and do well at school are going to do well in life.* And, conversely, people who mess around and do not do their work properly are going to suffer, not only now, but throughout their lives.

According to this story, the finest preparation for a good life is to be an A-grade student — and the quickest way to bring about ruin and disaster is to mess up your exams and regularly hand in your homework late.

You can see why this idea is extremely persuasive. In some ways, work is a bit like school. You have to go there every day, you can't just leave because you feel like it, there are people in charge and there are lots of rules. It stands to reason that someone who knows how to get along in a school environment is also probably going to fit in well in an office. Furthermore, many employers do pay a lot of attention to school and university results. It could be the first thing they look at when you send them a letter and explain who you are and why you would like to work in their company.

Nevertheless, it is not quite that simple... Sometimes, rather confusingly, we come across people who triumphed at school (they might have been prefects and won prizes and cups and been friends with the headmaster), but flunked in their work life. And vice versa. Some former school stars who once knew exactly how to satisfy their teachers may end up in a mediocre job, not doing anything particularly worthwhile or earning much money. At the same time, occasionally, the person who always did their homework late and would cheekily tell the teacher they found their class very boring might perform amazingly in their career: they may start a fast-food business that revolutionises healthy eating, or present fascinating television programmes or make a lot of money selling a new kind of computer — and no one asks them how they did in their high school French exam.

How could this happen? Is school important to success in later life? Or is your performance there utterly irrelevant in the grand scheme of things?

The first thing to say is that schools were not designed by people who necessarily have much experience of, or talent at, working life outside of school. Most teachers would have little clue how to do well in politics, business or science. They may be brilliant teachers, but even though they're supposedly training you for the big wide world, they don't have too much experience of this world themselves.

That helps to explain certain bad habits that schools may teach you (alongside some genuinely very valuable stuff), which we will talk about over the next few pages.

Tech Entrepreneur

Being a tech entrepreneur means spotting a problem and providing technological solutions. If you are really lucky you might get to meet a unicorn.

There's always a correct answer

Schools will generally teach you things that are already quite well known; and you will get good marks by repeating back to teachers ideas that they have carefully explained to you in the past. Whatever they may claim, most schools are not looking for you to be particularly original; they're asking you to repeat what you've been taught (about what happened in the Second World War, or how clouds are formed, or the best way to do quadratic equations).

However, at work, you will very often be faced with questions to which no one knows the answer yet. At a meeting, someone might ask, 'Should we open an office in South Korea?' This is a fundamentally different sort of question to a typical school challenge like 'Name three ways in which clouds can form'.

In the work example, there are not endless textbooks to refer to, there is not a curriculum, no one has been there before, so you have to think on your feet and come up with an intelligent guess. You might get asked, 'Who should we hire for our team?' And there is no right or wrong answer here either: it's about using your judgement in a deeply murky context.

But murky contexts aren't generally what school teaches you to deal with — the A-grade student who always knew the 'correct' answers to the questions set by the teacher may find themselves in serious difficulties.

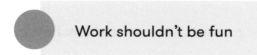

Don't break the rules

Schools will typically teach you to be obedient — and a good student is often defined as someone who follows rules. Some schools will talk a lot about how they want their students to be 'independent' and 'free thinkers'. But this is almost never true in any profound sense; it would simply be too difficult, and too chaotic, if four hundred pupils truly did start to think for themselves. It would be a mess. However, out there on the broad highway of life, you do — at carefully chosen points — have to break rules, ignore precedents, go against certain traditions and make some choices that may (for a time) shock or surprise respectable opinion. That requires a lot of inner strength — just the kind of strength that paradoxically won't endear you very much to the average history or geography teacher.

Work shouldn't be fun

School rewards a capacity for being bored, for not asking for too much fun, for suffering and for keeping going. That can be extremely handy in many parts of adult life too, but a good journey through the working world additionally requires you to be able to understand and follow your own passions.

Work done out of passion is always going to be better than work done out of duty and so — in a competitive world — success depends on identifying what you love in order to stand a chance of winning against other passion-driven contestants. If you're managing any kind of B2C business, you need to be able to put yourself in a customer's shoes and that means using your own sense of what is interesting, tasty, beautiful or good. Doing well at work requires you to ask a very distinctive question: *What is fun for me?* You need to bring yourself into the picture; pleasing 'the teacher' while shutting down your own pleasure centres is not enough.

People skills aren't necessary

It's an awkward truth, but doing well at school is compatible with not getting on with other people, aside from your teachers (who are in a very small minority). You could be thought of as unfriendly, grumpy, annoying and a real pain by everyone in the class and still win all the prizes. You can entirely lack what adults sometimes call 'people skills', and still do brilliantly.

In the workplace, however, people skills are indispensable; you can't survive in a work environment without being sensitive to the needs of others, charming customers and colleagues, being nice to people you don't like, finding out what those around you are worried about without upsetting them and admitting you might be wrong about something.

 Teaching isn't as important as learning

Schools deeply reward the art of being a good pupil: that is, being told what to do and listening well to the ideas of others. But adult life requires something even more difficult: being a good teacher. It's not that you'll literally have to be a school teacher, but you will need constantly to 'teach' other people — customers, colleagues and bosses — about important things: it won't be about trigonometry or the reign of Henry VIII, but more things like: 'why this kind of shampoo really is better for your hair and for the planet', and, 'why I think we should do another budget meeting on Tuesday mornings'.

In order to teach well, you will have to use all sorts of skills that good teachers will know about: a mixture of kindness and authority, charm and politeness, sympathy for those who don't yet see your point of view together with a capacity for gentle (and sometimes joke-filled) coaxing. The irony is that the one thing schools don't teach you is something that they so easily might: *the art of teaching*. So life requires you to do something very odd-sounding: to study your very best teachers, the ones

GREAT THINGS YOU WILL LEARN WHILE YOU ARE AT SCHOOL	EXTRA THINGS YOU MAY NEED TO PRACTISE FOR WORK
A host of ideas and skills, from English to maths and history to physics, that will be directly relevant in your work	How to think on your feet and come up with intelligent solutions when the answer isn't always very clear
A capacity for diligence, effort and endurance, which certainly has its place in the course of a working life	When is the right time to break rules, ignore precedents, go against traditions and make innovative decisions
A knowledge of how to please authority when you need to	A range of people skills like how to be sensitive to the needs of others and how to admit when you are wrong
An ability to be punctual, organised, and get things done to a deadline	Understanding what you love doing and how that can be turned into a job
Enthusiasm for tucking in your shirt and brushing your hair	Being a good teacher

everyone likes and would do anything for, and wonder what it is they're doing — and then copy it!

All this said, it is not the case that everything they teach you at school is nonsense and worth ignoring. That is a mistake as well. There are some extremely important things that you will be able to learn in your school years: new ideas and skills, diligence, effort and endurance, respect for authority, and how to be organised and punctual.

A good life requires us to do two very tricky things: to be an extremely hard-working student for many years at school, and at the same time, to be aware that school doesn't teach you everything, and that work will ask you to do things none of your teachers ever mentioned — things that may be closer to play and rebellion than duty and obedience. It's a balancing act — but we have every confidence you'll manage it.

Why do people end up in jobs they don't like?

S adly, quite a lot of adults end up in jobs they don't enjoy very much. They might not be terrible jobs — they could be jobs someone else would really like — but they're jobs that make these adults miserable. Let's think about a few reasons why this happens.

Excessive obedience

One of the hardest things to get right (as we have seen in the previous chapter) is to know when to submit to rules and when to rebel against them. Many adults end up miserable because they are too good at being obedient. They always do what is asked of them, even if it's a bit unreasonable and they would have been better off saying no.

When they were children, these adults might have had very frightening parents who were so strict that there was never any chance to say 'I don't quite agree...' They just had to do what they were told or else they got shouted at. This certainly made them 'good' boys or girls, but it stopped them from listening to and following their own hearts; that would have been too scary. As an adult, it's great to know how to be 'good'; it's even more important to know how to be yourself.

Excessive rebellion

There can also be a problem in the other direction, with adults who are simply too rebellious. Every time someone asks them to do something, they feel compelled to say no to assert their independence. They dislike any kind of authority, they're messy and unpunctual, and — in the end — impossible for companies to employ.

A bit of intelligent, quiet rebellion (the sort that doesn't get you into trouble and is compatible with being an agreeable person) is vital, but too much can eventually destroy your life. You can be yourself and still, at times, accept that you need to do exactly what you're told.

Falling in love with prestige

Some jobs carry very high prestige: they are generally seen as really good things to do. If you say you want to be a doctor or a lawyer or a scientist, no one is going to turn round and say 'That is a terrible thing to want to be'. These jobs have big salaries and a lot of respect attached to them.

The problem here has nothing to do with the actual jobs — they could be perfectly nice. The trouble is that prestige is not a good reason to choose a job that might not suit you. Prestige tricks our brains. It makes us think that because something is admired by other people, it's what we should do.

This is a problem that crops up around lots of different things. Imagine you could go anywhere on holiday. If you listen to what prestige says, you'd maybe decide to go skiing or to stay on a tropical island. But you might be different: you might actually prefer to go and stay with your grandmother or to go and see some industrial buildings that interest you. Other people might think that would be very boring — and perhaps it would be for them. But you're not trying to choose a holiday for someone else — you're trying to work out what it would be best for you to do.

It's the same with jobs. A prestige job could be right for you, but the fact that other people think it's a good job isn't really telling you what you need to know. You should be very careful about prestige.

Family

Your family is probably extremely interested in your happiness and what is 'good for you'. Nevertheless, families can cause particular problems when it comes to work. Though it is not meant in a sinister or nasty way, families can subtly influence the younger generation to do what they approve of and what they know about, rather than what would be interesting or good for the young person in question.

Almost certainly, a lot of what you think about work comes from your family. You might not notice this influence but your family will constantly be sending out little signals about what jobs are worthwhile, interesting or simply on their radar. What this may also mean is that lots of other kinds of jobs that might be good or interesting for you simply won't enter your mind, or they will not feel like an obvious choice, or they will seem like they are not possibilities for you. Your family's distinctive horizons might limit your own.

I'm not sure what I want to be when I grow up...

Why don't you be an engineer like your mum?

A way to get round this problem is to pay attention to it. Maybe you will be watching television and you might think 'I don't know anyone who works with animals but perhaps that's an interesting occupation'; or you could be shopping and look up and reflect: 'My family never mentioned anyone who makes the kind of lightbulbs you see in malls, the big powerful ones, and that might be an area to focus on one day...' You are reminding yourself of how big and varied the world of work really is — and of how many options have gone unmentioned by your family.

Too much competition

Some jobs sound amazing and are constantly spoken about by everyone: being a successful artist or a professional tennis player, a model or a singer... It is natural that when we start thinking about work, our thoughts might turn to these sorts of jobs.

But there is a problem: because so much attention is paid to these occupations, lots and lots of people want to do them — but actually there are only a few opportunities to go round. Let's think about what happens with tennis players. About 75 million people like to play tennis, but only a few hundred people actually make a living by playing in competitions. You could be a good player and practise very hard for years and years and still not end up being able to do it as a job.

It's the same with people who make money from online games. Huge numbers of people are interested in creating games like these, but hardly anyone makes money from it. Sometimes they make a lot of money very quickly, but it's extremely rare that this happens.

When a particular kind of job is over-subscribed, your abilities and your efforts are not likely to get a good reward. It is not because you are terrible at it, but because the competition is insanely tough. With the same effort you could probably be more successful (and more satisfied) doing something else.

Being happy at work means being really smart about the odds of success, sometimes avoiding the races in which there are too many competitors already — and concentrating on those that you can actually win.

Game Designer

Do you like to make up stories? Game designers can create whole new worlds, explore unknown galaxies or bend space and time. Combines creative wizardry with technical skill.

Sometimes our families can influence how we think about what we'd like to be when we grow up. Here are some questions to help you think about how your family approach work.

Once you've thought about work in relation to your family, then try answering the same sorts of questions for another family — maybe the family of a friend. You might not know all the answers, because you might not know your friend's family well enough. But even if you really don't know, you can try imagining the answers. They may be fascinatingly different and help you to get a wider perspective on the options open to you in the future.

What kinds of jobs do your family members do? Are they similar?

What kinds of jobs do your family talk about a lot or admire?

What kinds of jobs do your family not seem to like very much?

Do people in your family usually work for others or for themselves?

Is there a kind of job that they might think is a bit strange or not normal?

What do your family think about money? Could you consider it another way?

How to answer people who ask you what you are going to do

B y now, you will probably have acquired a lot of ideas about how you might answer the next well-meaning adult who comes up to you at a party and asks you what you want to do when you're older.

Firstly, you might compliment them on how interesting the question is — but then you might kindly and charmingly take them in a slightly different direction to the one that they were expecting. You might say that you really don't have a clear idea yet about what specific job you're going to do, but that that's OK because you feel it's more important to get a handle on what you enjoy than to be able to name a particular job.

You might explain that you love expressing yourself, or have a taste for helping other people or are thrilled by the idea of putting things in order (it may be pencils now, but warehouses or nations later).

You might along the way (if you're in the mood) remind the adult of how hard it is to find a 'good' job nowadays because it isn't enough just to make money, it's also a case of trying to find what you like — which hasn't been the case throughout history.

You could explain that you enjoy school, but that you do not confuse doing well at school with one day doing well at work — because the two are really very different. If the adult is in the mood, you might add that you don't know everything about the world of work, but that you're committed to learning more over the coming years, particularly in regards to professions that your own family might not be experts in.

Then you can politely ask them how they themselves navigated through the world of work.

Lastly, as your conversation draws to a close and you prepare to move on to far more important considerations (like what is for pudding), then you might tell the enquiring adult about an interesting book you recently read that helped to expand your ideas about work. You might tell them that it did not give you all the answers, but that it did something even more important: it got you thinking.

QUESTIONS TO ASK ADULTS ABOUT JOBS

What did they do when they were 22?

When did they work out what they wanted to do?

Have they ever considered any alternatives?
If so, what are they?

How happy are they with their working lives?

Do they have any advice? Or regrets...?

Notes for the future